THE GREAT INVESTMENT DESTINATION

BILLIONAIRES IN THE MAKING

HARIKUMAR KUNNATH

PRESENTS A PERFECT ANALYSIS OF AN EMERGING ECONOMY, AN IDEAL INVESTMENT DESTINATION WHERE YOU CAN INVEST AND MAKE YOUR FORTUNE NOW!!

Copyright © 2021 HARIKUMAR KUNNATH

All rights reserved

The characters and events portrayed in this book are fictitious. Any similarity to real persons, living or dead is coincidental and not intended by the author.

No part of this book may be reproduced, or stored in a retrieval system, or transmitted in any form or by any means, electronic, mechanical, photocopying, recording, or otherwise, without the written permission of the publisher

ISBN-13: 9798732020571
ISBN-10: 1477123456

Cover design by: Art Painter
Library of Congress Control Number: 2018675309
Printed in the United States of America

Preface

This book is about the emerging economic story of **INDIA** after the Covid-19 pandemic during the year 2020. The pandemic induced economic slowdown has had a devastating effect on major economies of the world. On the other hand, India managed this crisis in a much better way than expected, thanks to the economic scenario or base created by the government before the pandemic happened.

The Indian Government has targeted to become a **5 TRILLION DOLLER Economy** in the next 5 years from the level of $2.87 Trillion (year 2020). The growth plan envisaged is definitely a paradigm shift for the country as it is aiming to achieve almost double the growth achieved so far.

In the year 2020, the Foreign Direct Investment amounted to a whopping **$73 Billion** which is HISTORICALLY THE HIGHEST EVER fund flow to India even with the present pandemic situation which is handled properly by the government and appreciated by the people all over the world. Meanwhile, the International Monitory Fund has predicted that India will have a growth rate of **11.5%** for the year ending 2022 and the Moody`s have predicted a **13.7%** growth.

So what do these figures indicate? Well, it indicates that India is poised for better growth and high economic returns, and it is the right time for anyone to invest in India and grow along with the economic progress of the country. The transparent economic policies and the support from the Indian government have paved the way for investors to make it big. We can be sure that this country will produce more billionaires in the coming years than any part of the world.

Being the Pharmacy of the World, India has proved its mettle by providing vaccines to many countries thereby helping them in the fight against Covid-19. This goodwill gesture has helped India establish good diplomatic ties with other countries and has emerged as a powerful nation equipped to handle the challenges in this post pandemic era.

We have come across extraordinary Leaders, Politicians, Ministers and Bureaucrats who have contributed to India's growth and taken corrective actions from time to time. I acknowledge and appreciate their role in helping India to become an economic power now. Though I have not mentioned any names in this book, I have discussed the crucial issues and how those were resolved.

The economic dynamics of the world had changed after the World Wars I and II, Similarly the pandemic has had a drastic effect on the World economies and everyone is hoping for normalcy and to achieve financial stability.

I have analyzed the economic scenario in detail and presented my views on how and why someone needs to invest in India and the various possibilities of where and how they can grow with definite understanding.

Wish you good luck, keep reading!

Thank you

Harikumar Kunnath

Author of the Book "HOW TO SHAPE YOUR CAREER AFTER MBA"

ashamanagement@gmail.com

CONTENTS

- INTRODUCTION
- SOME VIEWS ON HISTORICAL DEVELOPMENTS
- THE STORY AFTER INDEPENDENCE
- PROTECTED ECONOMY TO LIBERALIZED
- THE ECONOMIC SCENARIO AFTER AND BEFORE LIBERLIZATION
- THE PERIOD FROM 2014 AND PRESENT
- TARGET BY THE YEAR 2025
- ATMANIRBHAR BHARAT ABHIYAAN [SELF RELIANT INDIA CAMPAIGN]
- BUDGET SUPPORT FOR THIRTEEN SELECTED SECTORS
- SOFTWARE INDUSTRIES
- HIGH POTENTIAL SECTORS
- TRAINING AND DEVELOPMENT

- COMPARISON OF ECNOMIC SCENARIO BASED ON GDP
- CHANGE IN APPROACH
- INVESTMENT OPTIONS
- ESTABLISHING NEW COMPANIES FOR PRODUCTION AND SERVICE
- SOCIAL MEDIA USER BASE IN INDIA AS OF 2020
- FINANCIAL SUPPORT
- PLACE OF BUSINESS
- HOW TO MOVE ON WITH THE IDEA
- MAKING OF BILLIONAIRES

INTRODUCTION

A country's real strength can be determined in the way it handles a crisis. The Indian government handled the Covid-19 pandemic, the economic crisis and also the Border issues effectively. This has been acknowledged by world leaders and has garnered respect from all the other countries of the world. India has initiated vaccination for its own people and has helped other countries as well, by providing vaccine to more than **85 countries.**

Before getting into details of the present situation it is better to understand some of the historical details which made India to grow economically. **THE FACTS AND FIGURES** need to be described in detail to understand what changes had happened over a period of time positively for this emerging economy. These details will give a right perspective of what all are the **OPPORTUNITES** available and where an investment can **GROW** within a short period.

SOME VIEWS ON HISTORICAL DEVELOPMENTS

The British ruled INDIA from 1858 to 1947 and the country became economically poor by the end of their rule.

Prior to British rule, India used to export spices, cotton textiles, raw silks, fabrics, wheat, sugar, pepper, opium, precious stones etc. In fact, people came to India in search of livelihoods, trade and commercial activities. All those people from abroad first came to do business and later ruled the country and the details are well known. With the horrendous exploitation under the British rule, Indian economy was adversely affected. The only good thing that came out of their rule is that they had set up certain institutions for their convenience in ruling this country such as

- Educational Institutions – This was developed to make use of cheap labor available in India – the Indians were educated and trained for clerical jobs, they were always treated with contempt by the British officers. But then, education was a big game changer. It inspired many enlightened minds to take up the fight for freedom from British rule.

- Infrastructure, Roads and Railways – This was developed to ensure better connectivity for British goods in all parts of the country, heavy taxes were charged on indigenous products which eventually ruined the competitiveness of Indian industries.

So by the time the British rule ended, all the indigenous industries had collapsed and the Indian economy had hit rock bottom. From such a low point, India has now reached a position where it is respected throughout the world for its high economic potential.

THE STORY AFTER INDEPENDENCE

After the freedom struggle, INDIA chose to become a Democratic country with a Federal structure, a combination of a strong central government and various state governments. Since there was lot of inequality in the Indian society at that time, our political leaders were more inclined towards socialism and obviously that reflected on the policies of the government. The government focused on developing the Agricultural sectors, industrial sectors and service sectors. To work out a proper action plan and start working, the Planning Commission was incorporated. By considering various aspects, the planning commission segregated the industries into two as **CAPITAL INTENSIVE SECTOR and LABOUR INTENSIVE** sector. The capital intensive sector was controlled by the government whereas the other sectors were operated by private entrepreneurs or organizations. It is important to note that the private enterprises were in nascent stage and only the government could take the lead in terms of capital intensive sectors.

PLANNING COMMISSION

The five year plans were worked out to ensure better quality of life for Indians with a focus on growth and development. We had gone through 12 five year plans up to the year of 2014 and this journey has been very difficult but somehow India managed to achieve a lot considering its economic condition post-independence.

From 1951 to 1956, the first plan focused on agriculture as the first priority for the government was to ensure the self sufficiency of food for its people. The second plan 1956 to 1961 was to focus on industries to generate employment. The subsequent plans focused on growth and there is no doubt that the base of the Indian economy was the first two five year plans.

The dams like Bhakra Nangal, Damodar valley and Hirakund were constructed for irrigation purpose and there were lot of small and medium irrigation facilities developed throughout the country. This was done to boost the agricultural sector where the crops mainly depend on rain fall and water is an important resource for agriculture.

There were more number of public sector steel plants, oil refineries, defense production units and many companies such as the Hindustan Machine Tools, Sindri Fertilizers Unit (Fertilizer Corporation of India Ltd), Chittaranjan Locomotive Works (CLW), Integral Coach Factory, Hindustan Antibiotics Ltd, CSIR-National Physical Laboratory started their operations.

The third five year plan focused on the defense sector in a big way since there were problems after the war with China. After that every five year plan focused on various sectors like education, health care based on the need and requirements. However it continued as protective economy with license and tariffs etc.

PROTECTED ECONOMY TO LIBERALIZED ECONOMY

The year 1991 saw a drastic change in policies of the government especially towards the economic activities of the country. Before 1991, India had a protected economy with strong control on tariff as well as licenses whereas other countries such as EUROPE, USA etc had liberalized their economy during 1970 and achieved the good economic growth. China also introduced – open door policy which resulted in large exports as their prices were lower compared to other currencies. India announced the liberalized policies as the Indian currencies were devalued during 1991 to the extent of 18% to compete with other countries. India was late but kept the pace as per the requirements. Thus, the country had to change its approach, resulting in a pro market and pro capitalistic inclination and this helped in promoting growth in the economy. There was an overall growth in the economy and we were on race till 2008 when the economic crisis happened all over the world. The stock markets crashed and it affected many people. Thankfully, Indian economic fundamentals were stabilized by that time and it ran through the crisis smoothly.

The software sector slowly started picking up from 2009 onwards and even though the growth was minimal we could see more opportunities coming our way. The Pharmaceuticals and automobile industries were also promoted to a great extent to increase the exports. The liberalization was the best thing to happen at the right time which moved the economy to greater heights.

THE ECONOMIC SCENARIO BEFORE AND AFTER LIBERALIZATION

People who were born in the 1950s, 1960s and 1970s are the luckiest group as they have witnessed India's development and transformation in every aspect. I will give few examples to give you an idea of how everything happened stage by stage.

Earlier, a simple facility such as getting the landline **TELEPHONE connection** used to take months and was difficult. The quality of service was also very bad in those times. Now days each and every one is connected with a mobile phone which now offers various other functions also. In fact, we have reached a stage where we are totally dependent on mobile phones. Certain mobile companies' motto or USP itself is ZERO complaints from customers. We came a long way in communication and over all development in this sector.

ELECTRICTY connection and power shortage was another major problem which people faced over a long period of time. Now, electricity has become an integral part of our lives be it home, office, factory or a hospital. Availability of electricity was a major breakthrough and has helped various sectors.

TELEVISION availability has also helped in developing communication and has become a major medium for both news and entertainment programs. The older generation had only the Radio for entertainment and news.

TWO WHEELERS were not easily available for purchase and people had to wait for years to get them. Very few companies were manufacturing during those periods. Nowadays, many companies are manufacturing two wheelers and they all have customers as the standard of living and demand has increased over a period of time.

The same is the case with **CARS and automobiles** where the waiting period used to be years and we had to choose between

Ambassador and Fiat mainly. But now we can see that so many different types of cars are available. Earlier, owning a car was for the super-rich people only but now cars are becoming affordable for all due to the increased demand and standard of living. The manufacturers are now making cars for every one as per their purchasing capacities or requirements. Owning a car has become a necessity than a luxury. Thus, the definition of a middle class family is slowly changing.

COOKING GAS was never available to many homes and they had to use the traditional firewood or kerosene. Now that has definitely changed.

More **WOMEN** are going to **work** which has generated over all development in revenue to homes as well for the country. This created more disposable income for a family and food joints, hotels as well as the money spend on transportation has increased. More number of offices came up and also the EDUCATIONAL INSTITUTIONS were increased.

The above mentioned changes happened due to the effects of liberalization and by lifting protectionism from the economy.

Earlier, women were confined to homes and most of them were denied education and career dreams. Nowadays we can see that more women are educated, working and are taking care of the family as well. The contribution of women as a part of the working population is immense and has helped in the economic development of this country. This has happened during the last few years due to the higher education as well as the change in perspective of the society.

THE PERIOD FROM 2014 TO PRESENT

We can term this period as the **GOLDEN PERIOD for development and growth** as many reforms were initiated. The government was bold enough to implement various policies and these initiatives helped to improve the efficiency level everywhere. It managed to create the discipline and accountability in government institutions and the fear amongst the non-performers. Overall, this has helped the Indian economy. Let's take a look at some of the steps taken by the government:

- The **PARALLEL ECONOMY** was a continuous problem in those days and during 2016, the government declared **DEMONETIZATION**. This created a drastic change in the system and instilled fear amongst the people who were corrupt and indulged in illegal practices. Demonetization helped in improving the digital payments system in many establishments. The fund flow to terrorist activities reduced or almost ended. Most of the illegal routes were restricted and over all the collection of taxes improved. Most importantly, this action was a clear message to all that the government is determined in dealing with wrong doers. This in turn developed a positive strength for the honest business people to invest and grow in a transparent economy.

- The **GST** was introduced in the year 2017 and this has provided the taxpayers a great relief in tracking their day to day business transactions. They need not hang on the sales tax offices for filing returns and a total transparent system was adopted. Whenever there is a revolutionary change, there will be people who oppose it either for their own benefit or they may be ignorant about the subject or just to get mileage in misleading public. All the above actions were implemented with many difficulties by the government.

- **The JAN DHAN ACCOUNT** for the poor were announced during 2014 under which zero balance accounts were created in banks all over India to help both rural and urban poor. This facilitated the government to directly transfer subsidies and pension to the needy, thereby making the whole process simple and effective.

- In the scheme **MGNREGA** which offers guaranteed work for the poor, some changes were made. The wages and the number of work days per year were increased to help more people.

- **DIGITAL INDIA** focused on bringing all establishments under the digital drive which helped in transparency and speedy action for sanctions and licenses.

- **INCOME TAX** rules were made people friendly and simplified, resulting in more number of people filing the returns. The income declaration scheme also fetched good results.

- **UJALA** scheme helped rural poor to access gas connection.

- **UDAY SCHEME** helped to make electricity available in remote areas of the country.

- **SMART CITIES PROJECTS** in different states have been initiated to focus on the overall development of a city and create more number of well-developed cities.

- **JAL JEEVAN MISSION** was initiated for safe drinking water in rural areas.

- **INFRASTRUCTURE** development happened in a big way after 2014 and many highways and roads were constructed, this in turn increased the easy movement of products across the country.

- Providing **VACCINES** to other countries as a goodwill gesture has received lot of appreciation. India has created a special place for itself in the world arena and has leveraged soft power effectively. The share market responded very well and the highest growth was recorded recently.

All the above mentioned changes has helped the population to aspire for more and increased the productivity and consumption, helping the economy to grow further.

NITI AAYOG FROM 2014 [National Institution for Transforming India]

The five year plans were replaced by the NITI Aayog with the Prime Minister as the Chairperson. The Regional council includes the Chief Ministers, Lt. Governors, and Ex Officio Members who have worked towards various policies.

- The plans envisaged include **AMRUT [Atal Mission for Rejuvenation and Urban Transformation]** addressing the basic needs of the population, Digital and agricultural reforms.

- The great thing happened is the change in attitude of the officials of the government along with the ministers and the leaders. The paradigm shift had happened since the new set of politicians who are only interested in good governance, corrupt free dealings and economic growth. The slogan **"SABKA SATH SABKA VIKAS"** [growth along with everyone] gaining ground all over including the federal states. Now the states are competing with each other for bringing industries to their states and there is lot of support for a new industry or an enterprise.

- As per World Bank Index the **EASE OF DOING BUSINESS** in India ranked from **142 in 2014 to 63 in 2020** and this will reduce further by the end of year 2021. This is mainly due to the change in attitude over all in the country and people are very much conscious for voting and electing the government which supports development in the country.

Ease of doing business is the best thing that can happen to any country. This is a change from the past as there were dynastic rulers and it is still happening in certain federal set up but will change since the sentiments of people is very clear for everyone. The main tragedy of the dynastic politics was corruption and lack of discipline in the developmental activities. This is ruled out now with stringent measures and more and more educated and honest people are joining politics to do something for the country.

The **CEO WORLD MAGAZINE** has ranked the Entrepreneur friendly countries based on various parameters and the list says it all:

COUNTRY - POINTS

- USA - 42.88
- GERMANY - 41.05
- UK - 35.08
- ISRAEL - 34.25
- UAE - 31.01
- POLAND - 29.75
- SPAIN - 29.01
- SWEDAN - 28.16
- INDIA - 25.47

This is just to mention that there is still a scope for the growth in the coming months. The same magazine had given the **HIGHEST RANK of 49** as per their parameters for the **LABOUR SKILLS** aspect which is **highest in the world**. This is an important point to be taken since the skilled employees are more in India than other countries of the world.

TARGET BY THE YEAR 2025: USD FIVE TRILLION ECONOMY

The government has set a target of becoming a $5 Trillion economy by the year 2025 and has envisaged various actions plans to achieve the target. Initially, this seemed to be achievable but then there are several factors that can impact the growth rate. For instance, the pandemic which happened in 2020 has changed the market scenario all over the world and it is a great setback for most of the countries for the time being. India is on its road to recovery and it is expected that this crisis can be managed by India.

The present economy size is 2.7 Trillion Dollars as of year 2020 and when the government is planning to achieve almost double the present size of the economy within FIVE years, more opportunities will be opened for investment for high growth rate. The government is committed to achieve target growth rate of 9 to 10 percent and has been working towards it. So, definitely this is a great opportunity for everyone to invest in India and create fortunes!!

OIL PRICE and the revenue generated in the last few years helped to reduce the interest burden as the borrowing has reduced considerably. This along with the revenue generated from other sources increased the spending levels for large infrastructure developments and defense sector.

DISINVESTMENT PLAN

Government is planning to disinvest large number of government companies with a target of achieving rupees 2.5 Lakh Crores and this is an excellent strategy. It is an ongoing process and there is a plan to disinvest around **300 government companies over a period of time by keeping only about 24** companies which are of strategic importance. The amount generated will be used for the developmental activities which will again generate revenue.

By doing this government is getting two benefits, one being the revenue to implement large infrastructure projects and the other one is increased efficiency in the organizations as there is a clear message from government that it is here to generate business growth and will not stick to loss making enterprises. This is a great opportunity for people to buy the shares and so every citizen can actually participate in the growth story.

AGRICULTURAL REFORMS

Government has just passed the new farm bill which was pending for a long time now. The present situation is that the agricultural lands are divided into small holding and there is no scope for them to make it in a big way unless and until huge capital is infused for development. The farmers are not getting the right price for the produce since the farmers are not organized and middlemen take major portion of the profit. Most of the produce is seasonal and perishable in nature so it is difficult for farmers to make profits.

Through the farm bill, the government wants to remove the middle men and address the problems of growth, harvest, storage, transport, procurement, processing and selling. To ensure the right price for the farmers we need large private investments that can help modernize the entire process through technology and machinery. These changes can be beneficial to farmers and help in improving their livelihoods.

The pre-harvest loss and the post-harvest loss were estimated to be in the range of SIXTY MILLION TONNES in a year, this is huge and the waste generated by this is at an alarming proportion. If the changes in policies are implemented it will benefit the economy in a big way in the coming years since large areas in India will come under proper cultivation. A great opportunity for anyone to enter and generate growth in the agricultural sector with modern farming which is the need of the hour as the main problems are seasonal variations, storage and price fluctuations. There will be an opportunity for exporting the products if a proper infrastructure is built with mass production.

SKILL INDIA

To address the growing need for employment, the government introduced the Skill India program for the youth to develop the skills of people to increase their employability. Many young people have undertaken the skill development programs and the total number of employable/skilled population have increased. This is a great asset for the nation since there will be more people who are job ready and can earn their livelihoods. Basically many feel that the present education does not makes the person job ready and the government is taking lot of initiatives for improving the basic skills. Since our country has a large part of educated young population, this initiative can generate employability, production and manufacturing.

START UP INDIA

We are hearing the Buzzword **"START UP"** very often as the central government is pushing for the same in order to **increase the employment generation** as well as for the well being of the people.

The problems and opportunities involved in starting a business is almost similar to that of the past as compared to now since the risks involved and the success rate percentage is almost same. However there is a push from government now days for the people to start the business as this can **increase the GDP** and the growth in our economy.

The government has created an atmosphere to support the small and medium enterprises in a big way as it can contribute to the GDP.

It is evident from the figures that the largest employers in India are in the **UNORGANIZED** sector. There are traders, hotel owners, shop and factory owners who employ laborers, daily wagers and small time service individuals. These employees have no job security and are totally dependent on the employers in the unorganized sector. So in times of crisis, this part of working population may completely lose their livelihoods. To remove this problem, the government is seeking to provide more help for the employers in the unorganized sector so that they can support their workers.

It is also important to note that employment generation in organized sectors are slow and will take time. However in the small scale sector it is immediate and functions well with income generation. With a view to increase the presence of more small scale sectors in the country the government have introduced MSME loan support scheme called **MUDRA LOAN**. There are three such types of schemes:

- Shishu = Loan upto Rs. 50,000/-.
- Kishore = Loan upto Rs.5, 00,000/-
- Tarun = Loan upto Rs.10,00,000/-

Many people have joined this scheme and have started their businesses and industries. Added to this there is support from the government in all respects for this from start to finish. The startup initiative is creating more number of successful entrepreneurs in the country now. The unorganized sector is actually helping the activities of the large sector by boosting the local manufacturing to a great extent.

ATMANIRBHAR BHARAT ABHIYAAN [SELF RELIANT INDIA CAMPAIGN]

The economic situation improved considerably along with the standard of living of the middle class in large numbers. The definition of middle class itself changed since most of the people are aspiring for better house hold facilities due to the high disposable income. There were times earlier when the percentage of daily food expense of any house hold were higher but now that is the lowest unless they go out for dining. It should be noted that there is an increase in purchasing power and the demand for **GOOD VALUE FOR MONEY PRODUCTS** has grown at a faster pace. The import from other countries has increased considerably. The **SELF RELIANT INDIA** move will give more opportunities for anyone who is planning to set up new ventures as per the products and services mentioned by the central government. The government has realized that many products that are imported due to convenience can easily be manufactured in India. This very thought of self-reliance is a game changer and this campaign is a major step towards generating businesses and jobs for our people.

The following figures will give you an idea of what is happening in the import front:

- **IMPORT VALUE** OF VARIOUS GOODS FROM OTHER COUNTRIES. [YEAR 2020 FIGURES]

- LARGEST FIVE [In Billion US Dollars]
    - CHINA - 58.71
    - USA - 26.89
    - UAE - 23.96
    - SAUDI - 17.73
    - IRAQ - 16.26

[REFERENCE - All figures were given in Lok Sabha by the minister]

With the above figures, it is clear that INDIA is importing large quantities of products from CHINA other than oil, arms and ammunition. The total import bill for the year 2020 is **371.98 $BILLION** and the above five countries contribute to **38.59%** of the total import.

The major imports from China now are as per the following:

- Telecom instruments
- Computer hardware and peripherals
- Fertilizers
- Electrical components and instruments
- Project goods
- Organic chemicals
- Bulk drugs

- Consumer electrical
- Electric machinery

All these products can be manufactured in India itself and so for obvious reasons the efforts have been taken by the government to manufacture here with proper incentives to enterprises. Added to that the ever growing domestic demands has to be met which will be huge in the coming years as high growth rate is expected which indicates high purchasing power and demand for products. So, for an investor these are excellent opportunities to taste success.

The balance of payments figures do not look favorable as the imports are increasing since most of the high value products are imported from other countries. In order to make India self-sufficient, the government announced the Atmanirbhar Bharat Abhiyaan and started concentrating on domestic production facilities. India is a country with large number of skilled people in all grades and so this initiative can benefit many people across the country.

As per the **MAKE IN INDIA** drive, the following sectors were mainly named after considering several aspects:

DEFENSE, SPACE, AVIATION, MINERALS, POWER, ATOMIC RESOURSES, SOCIAL INFRASTRUCTURE

Indian government started thinking on the lines that we as a country have the best minds, talent and skilled people along with appropriate resources then why can't we manufacture and increase our exports? This thought process has resulted in the push towards Make in India products and this is definitely going to boost the Indian economy.

DEFENSE

India is the **THIRD largest defense force** to spend after US and China.

To get an idea about the defense expenditure, I am placing the following table containing the details of the major countries of the world having the largest **DEFENSE BUDGET.**

Total Budget and GDP Percentage of Various Countries:

- USA - 732 Billion $ and 3.4% GDP
- CHINA - 261 Billion $ and 1.9% GDP
- INDIA - 71 Billion $ and 2.4% GDP
- RUSSIA - 65 Billion $ and 3.9% GDP
- SAUDI ARABIA - 61 Billion $ and 8% GDP
- FRANCE - 50 Billion $ and 1.9% GDP

- GERMANY - 49 Billion $ and 1.3% GDP
- UK - 48 Billion $ and 1.77% GDP
- Japan - 47 Billion $ and 0.9% GDP
- South Korea - 43 Billion $ and 2.7% GDP

India's Defense Expenditure

India was importing most of the products from other countries and since the import bill was going up to very high percentage, it is a big burden on the government.

So the Indian government has planned to manufacture most of the items in India itself and the private players will have a larger role to play now.

Why the spending levels are more for defense?

The world has changed a lot from the olden thinking of "expansionist" theory where the Kings or Rajas conquer places with their might and occupy territories of other countries. This kind of attitude was changed after the world wars and there is stability all over except for few incidents. There are certain forces or countries that still believe in the expansionist theories and are compelling other nations to increase their defense outlay. There are also countries which support terrorist activities and unfortunately this is continuing in spite of lot of discussions and efforts. The military spending is inevitable for the survival of any country with these kinds of circumstances.

The Indian government has now decided to create a manufacturing base for defense products with private players in the country. This is a very huge investment opportunity and it will increase the manufacturing activities to a great extent along with employment generation. India has already started exporting to over 40 countries and the number will go up in months to come. This is a great opportunity for any large or medium organizations to venture into some manufacturing sector which is complementing the defense production. Even a small manufacturer can contribute and make high turnover if they manage to get in as the suppliers to this big industry.

AVIATION

Aviation in general got expanded and it became affordable to most of the middle class people, thanks to the low cost airline started by Air Deccan earlier. Now the government wanted to get out from the AIR INDIA which is government of India entity. All these government companies have huge assets like real estate, infrastructure etc and the only thing that needs to be available is the working capital flow. If that is generated by private entities, we can get be assured of profitability.

All the other sectors kept for disinvestment are equally important for the purpose of investment and growth. The idea of the government is to turn India into a **WORLD MANUFACTURING HUB** in the near future which is very much possible with the support and infrastructure development.

BUDGET SUPPORT FOR THIRTEEN SELECTED SECTORS

The central government recently announced a scheme and budget amounting to **TWO TRILLION DOLLARS for 13 industries** as a production linked incentive which is over a period of time. This will be in the range of 4 to 6 percent to the following products categories - BULK DRUGS, MEDICAL DEVICES, AUTO COMPONENTS, TEXTILES, FOOD PROCESSING, BATTERY STORAGE, SOLAR PHOTOVOLTAICS, TELECOM AND NETWORKING PRODUCTS AND WHITE GOODS. It is very clear that the government intention is to reduce the dependence on other courtiers for various products and the import has to be reduced. In the above mentioned categories, Bulk drugs are important as India is one of the largest exporters of medicine to the world. This is a great opportunity for a business group to enter and establish its presence. In months to come, India will surely become the largest manufacturing hub in the world as required infrastructure and facilities are being developed on a war footing now with great clarity.

With all this government planning and communication, there is a general awareness everywhere that the major thrust is towards developmental activates and many people will be benefitted. This in turn developed a healthy competition between the federal states to attract more investors with competing facilities. These things are also featuring in the election manifesto from time to time at the time of state elections. Now more states are seeking to have large number of industries in their area. The main states which are in the front run are UTHAR PRADESH, MAHARASTRA, HARYANA, RAJASTHAN, ANDHRA PRADESH, TELANGANA, TAMIL NADU AND KARANATAKA. All these states have developed infrastructure to accommodate more number of industries. The number of startups in these states has also increased.

A research paper recently published by CREDIT SUISSE GROUP (financial services company) mentioned that already there are about more than **100 BILLION DOLLAR WORTH UNLISTED COMPANIES** in India which are all NEW VENTURES. There are around **1000 OR MORE VENTURE CAPITALISTS** who are available for supporting the right idea of business in India. Basically, the investors look for the right idea and drive to work hard as all the other necessary components/resources can be facilitated. The next few years will be a growth story and those who are participating now can make their fortune.

SOFTWARE INDUSTRIES

The IT export as of 2020 is 150 Billion US dollars and domestic consumption is around 45 Billion US dollars. [TOTAL OF **US$195 Billion**] This is going to become a major drive force for export in the coming months. There are opportunities available in the area of SAAS, CLOUD COMPUTING, ARTIFICIAL INTELLIGENCE, SECURITY, EDGE COMPUTING, BLOCK CHAIN, INTERNET OF THINGS, 3D PRINTING, VERTUAL REALITY AND MACHINE LEARNING. There are many more allied services that are coming along with this industry. Indian skill in this sector is greatest in the world and many more companies are coming forward in investing the country since all the infrastructures are in place and there is good support from government side. The institutions that are teaching software and imparting IT knowledge have increased and these institutions are providing education along with skill oriented programs. The tremendous skills and knowledge of professionals in India and the availability of manpower in various stages is more than sufficient for any organization to start their ventures.

The software industry is moving upward continuously and it was not affected even with the pandemic. In fact it is the only industry which was quick to bounce back and handle the situation by arranging the Work From Home [WFH] options and actually turned the crisis to an opportunity. Some companies reported more effectiveness and also less expense by cutting costs for the rent, electricity, transport and other facilities. The change in world economic scenario is also helping India, it is easier and acceptable to operate from any place and this is beneficial for businesses as a whole and more companies are starting or shifting their base for lower costs.

We can expect another boom in this industry within a couple of years. The quantum computer will make changes in the working of software and data science in the coming years. The **Deep Tech Club of NASSCOM** is helping the start up ventures in the field of quantum computing which is a welcome change. There are more than 80 ventures in deep tech club and this will definitely change the future of the industry as a whole with lot of innovative ideas and plans. There can be more incubators for research and development in the coming months and this is an opportunity to invest and make innovative changes in the industry. The pioneers will be benefitted in the long run.

HIGH POTENTIAL SECTORS

Let us discuss some of the sectors that have high potential and have shown tremendous growth.

EDUTECH

Another sun shine industry is the EDUTECH and this is moving in astronomical proportions since most of learning can be done by sitting at your home only. The pandemic has given an extra opportunity and this will become a norm for the future course of learning. Many companies have started and they have established their brands and attracted huge investments from India and abroad. This is going to stay and there will be more innovations which will take place during the future course of action. Huge investments are happening and definitely a new area of innovation will happen in future with multiplicity of various activities.

The greatest achievement through this revolution is that anyone, even in a remote village or small cities can learn better courses which were earlier available only in major cities through offline class rooms. The internet penetration levels have also increased along with the online education. The startup BYJUS in education started only in the year 2011 and now it is valued at US$14 Billion and attracting more number of investors from all over the world. There are others like UNACADEMY; VEDANTU etc which are also growing at a faster pace. It is expected that there will be lots of learning opportunities for people across the world and you can learn almost everything under the sun through online classes. So there is enough scope for growth and innovation in this sector.

PHARMA PRODUCTS

The Pharmaceutical industry will grow to US$100 Billion in the year 2025 and the medical device will grow to US$25 Billion. This is the growth expected by the government of India and the opportunities available for the investments are huge. The government of India **allowed 100% FDI** for the industry and already the signs of growth have registered. The vast growing population requires the medicines regularly due to the change in environment and health issues related to the old age etc. This is also a great opportunity for India to increase the exports as there is a pricing advantage in comparison to other countries.

India is now becoming a pharmacy of the world by manufacturing many number medicines and vaccines which are catered to local as well as for foreign countries. This is a large turnover business now for the private pharmacy companies in India as the consumption/demand for various types of medicinal drugs is very much there. Manufacturing of bulk drugs of certain category will also be beneficial as India used to import huge quantity from China.

The specialty hospitals are also increasing and there are patients coming from neighboring countries for better treatment since the facilities are more in India. This is also another opportunity for establishing new specialized hospitals and developing latest healthcare infrastructure to cater to the increasing demands.

AUTOMOBILES

There are already large number of automobile manufacturers of different brands and sizes in India. There is a great demand in domestic market itself since large number of middle class is purchasing the vehicles for their use. The first time buyers are more and it is in an encouraging stage for every manufacturer. Added to that there is export happening and this will continue to more number of countries in the coming years since the development of electric vehicles. The world leader TESLA already started their operations in India and the government is supporting this since this can reduce import of oils. Automobile sector is also a great opportunity for investment.

E-COMMERCE

The pandemic created a strong base for the E-commerce industries and according to the figures available through media the growth rate has just doubled from the previous year. The main reason is that less people are moving out of the house and they are exploring the possibilities of getting things at their door step. Even though this facility was available earlier, it was only during the pandemic that its potential for growth was fully realized. Especially during the last few months the e-commerce industry has grown steadily. This is going to last long since many new customers have joined and it is also a matter of convenience of sitting at home and it has become the new normal to shop most items from online.

There are many names in this field like Amazon, Big Basket, Grofers, Myntra, Flipkart, Alibaba, India mart, Snapdeal, Book my show, 1MG, First city, Nykaa, Ebay etc. There is a great opportunity in this area since the internet penetration level is not uniform even though the internet facilities are available in more areas now. This sector definitely has high potential and can be developed further.

TOYS MANUFACTURING

In India, the toy industry is growing very fast and most of it is in the unorganized sector. There is room for great brands to organize and make it very big in coming years. This is going to change and will be a global manufacturing place in months to come as more people are venturing into this sector.

RENEWABLE ENERGY

This is an area where there is a great scope for the development since the government itself is supporting for it. Given the threat of climate change, most nations are looking for solutions to make optimum use of renewable resources. The various types of renewable energy are as per the following:

- SOLAR
- WND
- THERMAL

Solar energy can be useful for every one as the entire world is seeking to have an extra source as an alternative to electricity. Many people are now using solar power at home along with electricity. Since electricity consumption is increasing day by day, maximum utilization of this resource can cut many costs. There are some organizations which are making use of solar energy but there is still scope for more development.

Wind energy is also being used by certain states in India and it is developing in a big way. Government is also keen to support environment-friendly endeavors and will be providing subsidies.

TRAINING AND DEVELOPMENT

Training is an integral part of development and the government has been taking efforts to boost educational institutions, this is definitely a good sign for investment opportunity.

PRESTIGIOUS EDUCATIONAL INSTITUTIONS

There is an overall improvement in education during the last few years and the details of the number of PREMIUM AND PRESTIGIOUS higher educational institutions at present functioning are as follows. All these increased to the current level during the past 8 years.

- ALL INDIA INSTITUTE OF MEDICAL SCIENCES (AIIMS) - 22
- INDAN INSTITUTE OF TECHNOLEDGY (IIT) - 23

- INIDAN INSTITUTE OF MANAGEMENT (IIM) - 20

There are enough professional colleges all over the country and latest technical education are imparted through various institutions. The government is committed to improve the employability of the students and is also focusing on the entrepreneurship education. There will be no dearth of skilled people in any given time as learning has become accessible to all.

In large number of the states in India, the education at all levels have increased and more people have moved to white collar jobs resulting in the dearth of blue collar jobs in the above mentioned states. This resulted in movement of people from certain states where the education levels are low and filled the blue collar category quickly. This has triggered movement from the states of West Bengal and Bihar to other states and they found proper jobs in other places mainly in southern states. The jobs requirements will change from time to time and the remuneration will also increase over a period of time depending upon the growth and prosperity.

YOUNG WORKING POPULATION

India is having a large working population compared to other countries in the world which indicates that there are enough people for employment i.e. Human resources are more here and can be put to use. Many years back there were problems of unemployment in India and now everyone is finding jobs of their own choice if they are competent and employable. This is a welcome change and with the growth of many organizations the job opportunities will also increase.

COMPARISON OF ECONOMIC SCENARIO BASED ON GDP

To understand the details of the present economy of different countries we have to study the GDP figure of the current year. With the help of GDP, we can get an idea of WHAT WILL HAPPEN IN NEXT FEW YEARS in terms of economic development which is depended on the activities currently happening and the government policies of every country.

GDP OF COUNTRIES ($TRILLION)

- USA - 21.43
- CHINA - 14.34
- JAPAN - 5.08
- GERMANY - 3.86
- INDIA - 2.87
- UK - 2.83

- FRANCE - 2.72
- ITALY - 2.00
- BRAZIL - 1.84
- CANADA - 1.74

[Reference – Investopedia]

The opportunities will be more for business only if countries aim to achieve HIGHEST GROWTH and work towards it, India is certainly coming to the TOP as per the growth plan percentage.

CHANGE IN APPROACH

We have learned from the past that after every crisis in the world there will be change in the economic set up or the strength of the countries may differ due to the internal factors. This had happened after the world wars and some of the countries flourished and Japan is a perfect example. Their success became possible due to the efforts made by the government at that time and the effective work done by them. It is to be noted that the government policies will contribute to a great extend in development. During the periods 1970s and 1980s the Japanese government focused on export and improved their position as well as domestic consumption. The total attitude change was a boom for the country.

The same is the case with Singapore when they planned the growth after 1987. With the support of the government they grew faster and became a self-sufficient country. This is the story of many countries where if a strong central government and a right leadership operates can make development possible.

The time is ripe for India where everything is set for continuous growth in years to come. It is important to note that the entire mood of the nation has been changed to **"FOR THE DEVELOPMENT"** than any other focus. Even during elections the parties are promising the growth and welfare for the people than any other thing. This is good thing to happen along with activities of the government to support for the business development which is through private participation.

QUAD [Quadrilateral Security Dialogue]

The association formed between the four major countries of the world like **INDIA, AUSTRALIA, JAPAN AND USA** for security reasons is actually emerging to be a major force to reckon with for further tie up with all other activities. The economic cooperation due to the changed scenario of the world is also compelling this formation to look for other areas which are in common nature and this has become advantage for the entire world as a whole. This cooperation is definitely going to boost the trade between these countries as well as overall growth.

INVESTMENT OPTIONS

There are various opportunities available for starting the business in India in the categories mentioned in the previous chapters. The total investment options can be divided into four parts broadly for classification purpose:

- Creating large manufacturing companies for ARMS AND AMMUNITION FOR DEFENSE, SPACE, AVIATION, MINERALS, POWER, ATOMIC RESOURCES AND INFRASTRUCTURE

- Investing in the SHARES OF LARGE GOVERNMENT COMPANIES which are diluting the shares

- CREATING MANUFACTURING BASE for the products which are now imported largely from China and other countries

- Creating companies for the DOMESTIC CONSUMPTION for various products

NOW LET US ANALYZE EACH ONE OF THE ABOVE CATEGORIES:

- The first category needs the licenses and sanctions by the central governmental agencies and there are right policies laid out for the process. The idea of the government is not only to reduce the import but also to increase the supply to other countries. This needs huge capital and the bigger corporations can play an important role, they can create the turnover and generate employment.

- Large number of GOVERNMENT COMPANIES is to be sold or diluted in the coming months. There are number of government controlled BANKS to be privatized over a period of time. This is a great opportunity for any one with small or big investment to acquire the shares and be a part of the growth. It is known to all that the efficiency level of the private enterprises is much higher as they focus on profitability over a period of time in functioning and the turnaround is possible with in short periods. Added to that most of the government companies are having large amount of fixed assets which are not utilized. With a view to scale up the government companies large amount of investment is needed and it can be done only through the share offer to public as well as financial institutions. This is only change in ownership pattern and it is still owned by the public at large since the shares will be diluted to large number of people. There will be a focus on effectiveness basically because every company will become autonomous in nature without any political interference.

- Nowadays large number of working population are having more disposable income and they are investing in shares and that is one of the reason the Sensex and Nifty are on the higher side for the past few months even though the pandemic created a havoc in between. All the banks are having a product called SIP – Systematic Investment Plan and this gathered huge amount for investing in mutual funds. There is enough cash with every one for investing in shares and the all the IPOS recently are oversubscribed. One must watch and keep investing in shares directly or through the mutual funds. The companies which are showing positive side can bring funds by way of public participation through shares as per the guidelines of SEBI. This is a great opportunity for everyone to keep investing from time to time as per the availability of funds with them at any intervals.

- There are many of products which were imported from China and this is a great opportunity to come forward and invest in India for the local manufacturing and consumption. The details of these products are given in previous chapters. The dynamics changed and already lot of companies have shifted their base to India recently and they are finding it easy since both central and state government are creating single window clearing and the procedures are very quick these days. The mobile phones and accessories are the main product that needs immediate attention as this is imported in huge numbers.

- The computer hardware and accessories can also be focused for mass production. Even Electrical goods manufacturing need to be taken up on priority.

- Food processing is another area which is becoming a need. It is necessary to store and process seasonal products. White goods have already taken a place for manufacturing however any new addition can be thought of for catering to the domestic markets.

ESTABLISHING NEW COMPANIES FOR PRODUCTION AND SERVICES

There are various opportunities for the products to be manufactured for local consumption and export. We can divide this into two categories:

- New Concept
- Existing One

In the case of new concept, proper research needs to be done before getting into the production even if the economic situation is good. We have to take information right from the end consumer to the first buyer for any research. Once we have a new concept whether it is working very well abroad or if it is a new invention altogether it must be tested very carefully. The best idea here is to get a feeling from the end consumer itself through a well described research format and that has to be tabulated properly. If the concept is appealing to the customers then manufacturing can be done in a small way to test the pulse with modifications received from the findings. This can go further by doing test marketing in a geographically small market which is representing the pulse to make correct positioning to proceed further.

In an existing one, the risk is little less in finding the position. The entrepreneur or the company only needs to collect the data such as the total market size, pricing, packaging and market segmentation. There can be again a research from the consumer point of view for the changes that needs to be incorporated for the products or services. It is always better to change the products or service at this period than later as the expenses involved will be much more at a later stage.

The following are the main things that need to be taken care when you are starting your production for any existing products category which are already available in the market:

- Your Product must be different from the existing one in terms of more benefits

It is to be noted that there must be a differentiation in terms of the quality, price or packaging from the existing products by asking questions such as why a consumer should buy this since others are also available in the market. This can be found out by a research with the consumer itself since their requirements will change as per the time for any given product.

- Cost for manufacturing and products

The cost need to be taken into consideration after going through the factors of production since always the cost advantage wins the race. The main challenges in this area are the minimum purchase quantity of raw materials in any given time. This will tamper the new companies to stock large quantities of raw materials which are not required for production at a particular point in time. The only solution is to scale up the business to the next level or find a way to get the materials at a lowest price and one needs to be very careful since cutting corners will affect the overall quality of the products.

- New ideas and innovation

Need to identify the week points in the existing products or services and find out solution to that by regular innovative ideas. This is an important area in which any company can make a dent in the growth with new ideas and findings in existing products in the competition.

- More planning and understanding is required

- It is not easy for a start up to function and grow since the percentage of failures is more due to the lack of proper research and ability to understand the market situation correctly. There must be a combination of experienced people and the knowledgeable people in the organization and care must be taken to recruit the right people for the right job. Need to follow the best practices in the organization since the credibility is to be established through out without fail in the market and outside. There must be continued efforts to create good will for the organization which will only help in the long run. Cutting corners will damage the image which will affect badly to all functions. There is always room for improving the best practices comparing from the similar organizations which will be a plus point to get more share and grow faster.

- Always there must be a plan for getting share from competitors with new strategies continuously and this must continue as long as you are in business. There must be an update of competitors' activities to counter since the industry is vibrant and it is growing in very dynamic situation.

- There must be a continuous process whereby the financial health of the organization in monitored closely with the different financial ratios. This is important to understand and change the course of action if necessary from time to time. The satisfied employees are the greatest asset for any organization and this need not be only through the monitory benefits which they enjoy but also the other motivation factors. A highly motivated team is the success of any organization and you can vouch this by seeing the growth of any organization which is of dynamic nature. The CEO who is managing needs to be careful in selecting the right people for the organization.

- The advertisement channels have changed a lot during the last few years and the influence of the social media is to be taken into consideration. In the next chapter, I will be listing the penetration level of social media in India.

SOCIAL MEDIA USER BASE IN INDIA AS OF 2020

ALL IN CRORES

- WHATSAPP - 53
- YOUTUBE - 45
- FACEBOOK - 41
- INSTAGRAM - 21
- TWITTER - 2

The influence created amongst the public is an effective tool for business and the results can be achieved immediately. There are various types of media support and it can be selected as per the ratio of cost to the turnover or profit.

INVEST IN EXISTING COMPANIES

Another great idea is to invest in existing companies which are in need of dilution by attaining some strength. There are great brands developed by the promoters and investing in them will benefit in the long run as the country is progressing. We have seen a lot of investment happening in big brands even during the global economic slowdown due to the pandemic.

Small companies

There are also small brands and companies which need capital to scale up and some of them are ready for take over which have lot of potential in the long run. These are all great opportunities in India which is positive in terms of economic development.

FINANCIAL SUPPORT

The central government has passed a bill in the parliament recently in establishing a DEVELOPMENT FINANCE INSTTUTION **[DFI]** for sustaining support as a provider, enabler and catalyst for infrastructure financing with a capital of TWENTY THOUSAND CRORES with a lending target of **FIVE LAKH CRORES** within three years. This is a large support happening in India in terms of support and will change the course for an immediate development.

The interest rates are low and the banks are willing to support the startups and the large businesses if all the other parameters are right. In the past there has been lot of political influence on the banks which had shunted development but now the scenario is completely different. The change in the control system placed on banks and financial institutions has helped them perform better. Anyone who is genuine will be supported by the system itself which is a welcome change.

There was a time when the bank interest used to be around 24% per annum and the cost of production and manufacturing expense were at high level. Luckily, things have changed over a period of time. Now the banks are open for more amounts of credit as well as offer lower interest rates which are beneficial for entrepreneurs and conducive for business.

The corporate tax for companies has been reduced to the minimum. Currently the tax structures are only 22% and with the surcharge it will come to only about 25.17% whereas for new comers it is 15% and by including the surcharge it will come to around 17.16% which is one of the lowest in comparison to other countries. This is an encouraging factor for the companies to start their business in India and operate further.

PLACE OF BUSINESS – ANY WHERE IN INDIA

The infrastructure is being developed at a fast pace all over India including the small towns and villages, so any company that wants to shift can choose any place in India. Operating business from remote locations is now possible with the availability of infrastructure.

Nowadays the companies are not concentrated to main cities as many are moving out to small towns or moved already. The road and rail transport is increasing day by day for the connectivity to remote places as per the policy of the government. The electricity is available in almost every part of the country. Added to that is the INTERNET availability at the required speed in every village and town, this has indeed increased the level of education and opportunities for more people.

Most of the software companies have started moving out to smaller towns to reduce the cost and they have developed those small towns into areas of job availability and purchasing power. Educated skilled people are available everywhere as the educational institutions are scattered all over the places and those who are moving to these towns find it easy to get the right people for the right job.

There is a great amount of information available to any person with a minimum qualification due to the internet penetration and it is helping the overall population. Now everyone understands the need of the development through private enterprises and this is changing the ideology of the politicians also to a great extent for investment and growth for all.

HOW TO MOVE ON WITH THE IDEA

If the investment options are high and strategic then it is better to get in touch with the Central governmental institutions directly as there are dedicated offices in the ministry for single window clearance.

The organization or the individual can contact the respective chief minister's office of the state also for the clearance and establishment procedures. Every state now wants to get the industries to start in their own area and there is a healthy competition. After the 2020 pandemic, many companies have already shifted their functions to India and some are in the process. Most companies are coming from China and they have both the opportunity of getting the local markets for supply as well as the export market.

If the plan is to start an SME then there are great opportunities and one only needs to contact the local consultants or chartered accountants who are available even in smaller towns. They will take care of the sanctions and licenses with in less time.

START UPS IN THE NEWS

There are many number of successful start ups in India and some of the companies with the valuation as of 2020 are given below:

Company Name (Year of formation) – Current Valuation

InMobi (2007) - US$1.6 Billion

Swiggy (2014) - US$3.3 Billion

Flipkart (2007) - US$ 24 Billion

Freshworks (2010) - US$ 1.5 Billion

Paytm (2010) - US$ 16 Billion

DELHIVERY (2011) - US$ 1.6 Billion

Dream 11 (2011) - US$ 1 Billion

We can note the changes happening in the industry as the business opportunities are available in India for the last ten years and there are also many small companies which have made their presence with good turnover and profit during these years. With proper study of the market condition and the customer needs from time to time will be a factor determining the products or services required. Many entrepreneurs have created success stories to tell and many more are in the pipeline to establish their presence felt.

MAKING OF BILLIONAIRES

The communists' country like China also changed the ideology from all in government enterprises to including some private companies after the opening up from 1970 and added more than **known THOUSAND BILLIONAIRES** with in a gap of few years. They moved with the time and changed the ideology for development as per the situation which became a great stepping stone for their growth.

In India, the real focused development started from 2014 and it is continuing now with great strength as mentioned in previous chapters. These developments are taking place not only at the central governmental level but also at every federal state.

This is the right time to participate in the growth of this country through various capacities and within next few years you can see a different India altogether with fast economic development. This is a rare scenario where a country is aiming to double its GDP growth rate with utmost sincerity, hard work and quick decisions. This is indeed a **GOLDEN OPPORTUNITY FOR INVESTORS** to make it big, so we must use it in the best possible way. If China can produce more than thousand known billionaires then India can produce much more billionaires. In this **LAND OF OPPORTUNITIES – INDIA, BILLIONAIRES ARE IN THE MAKING**…just wait and watch!

www.ingramcontent.com/pod-product-compliance
Lightning Source LLC
Chambersburg PA
CBHW050247220526
45465CB00002B/580